EXCITING

singapore

a visual journey

Welcome to Singapore,
the dynamic island nation
where East meets West.

PERIPLUS

EXCITING
singapore
a visual journey

O N THE SURFACE, Singapore appears to be a brash, modern city just like many in the West. Yet beneath this veneer you will find a fascinating blend of Asian cultures. It is a nation at a crossroads, as Stamford Raffles recognised when he in effect colonised Singapore for the British in the nineteenth century. He turned the island into a thriving trading post between East and West. Mass migrations from China and elsewhere further transformed Singapore. After the Second World War and the Japanese invasion, the British granted Singapore self-governance in 1959. An attempt in 1963 to merge with Malaysia failed due to the regional tensions the alliance created, so in 1965 Singapore became an independent nation. Strong leadership led to modern Singapore: safe, clean, successful; a wealthy little country with a big reputation.

Contents

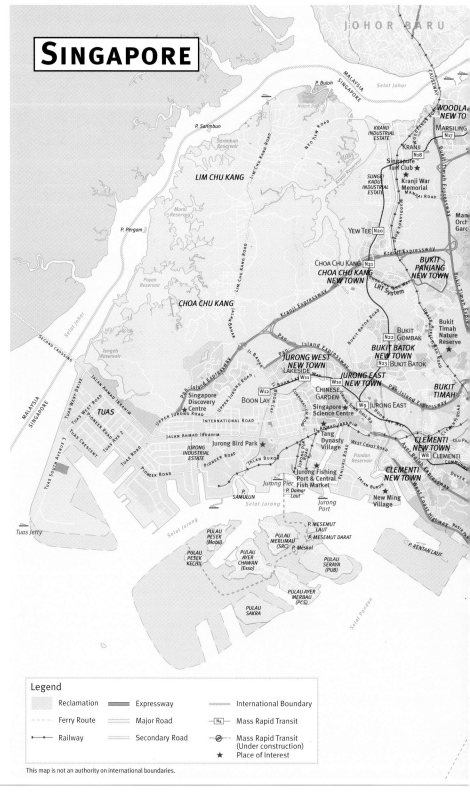

SINGAPORE

Legend

Reclamation	Expressway	International Boundary
Ferry Route	Major Road	N4 Mass Rapid Transit
Railway	Secondary Road	Mass Rapid Transit (Under construction)
		★ Place of Interest

This map is not an authority on international boundaries.

18

22

26

30

34

38

42

Sembawang
Shipyard

MALAYSIA
SINGAPORE

SENOKO
INDUSTRIAL
ESTATE

SEMBAWANG

Sembawang

N14

N15

ADMIRALTY

NDS

N12 Yishun
**YISHUN
NEW TOWN**

N11 KHATIB

MANDAI AVE

Lower
Selatar
Reservoir

ngapore
oological
ardens

**NEE
SOON**

Viewing
Tower

Upper
Selatar
Reservoir

PULAU
PUNGGOL
BARAT

PULAU
PUNGGOL
TIMOR

Punggol
Holiday
Camp

PUNGGOL

Punggol Fishing Port
& Wholesale Fish
Market

PULAU
SERANGOON
(Coney Island)

PULAU
KETAM

PULAU UBIN

Pulau Ubin

Serangoon Harbour

Changi Beach

CAFHI Jetty

JALAN KAYU

Tampines Expressway

Changi
Village

CHANGI

Changi Ferry
Terminal

YIO CHU KANG

N10

Yio Chu Kang

ANG MO KIO AVE 5

**HOUGANG
NEW TOWN**

**PASIR RIS
NEW TOWN**

Chalets &
Resort

LOYANG

Ang Mo Kio

N9

**ANG MO KIO
NEW TOWN**

**SERANGOON
NEW TOWN**

E12 Pasir Ris
Fishing

Tampines Expressway

THOMSON

Fishing

Upper
Peirce
Reservoir

Lower
Peirce
Reservoir

**BISHAN
NEW TOWN**

Bishan

N8

PAYA LEBAR

Crocodile
Farm

**TAMPINES
NEW TOWN**

E11 TAMPINES

Tampines Ave 7

Singapore Changi Airport

MacRitchie
Reservoir Park

Braddell

N7

**TOA PAYOH
NEW TOWN**

Toa Payoh

N6

E10 SIMEI

**SIMEI
NEW TOWN**

Bedok
Reservoir

Novena

N5

**JALAN
EUNOS
ESTATE**

KEMBANGAN

E8

**BEDOK
NEW TOWN**

E9

TANAH
MERAH

Newton

N4

LAVENDER E3

KALLANG

E5

E6

E7

Botanic
Gardens

Holland
Village

COMMONWEALTH

ORCHARD N3

BUGIS E2

Malay
Village

AJUNIED E4

GEYLANG

EUNOS

KATONG

**BEDOK
NEW TOWN**

Tanah Merah
Ferry Terminal

W6

Holland
Rd

SOMERSET N2

N1

**QUEENSTOWN
NEW TOWN**

W5

DHOBY GHAUT C2

TIONG
BAHRU

PAYA
LEBAR

Upper East Coast Road

East Coast Parkway

REDHILL W3

CITY HALL

OLD KALLANG
AIRPORT
ESTATE

EAST COAST ROAD

MARINE PARADE RD

ALEXANDRA RD W4

TANJONG
RHU

East Coast Parkway

Bedok Jetty

WG

TELOK
BLANGAH

QUTRAM PARK W2

RAFFLES PLACE C1

TANJONG PAGAR M1

East Coast Park

East Coast Park

Alkaff
Mansion

Mt.
Faber

MARINA
BAY

Singapore
Crocodilarium

World Trade Centre

Keppel East
Wharf

**PULAU
BRANI**

SENTOSA

SEE INSET

Cable Car
Towers

P. KEPPEL

Exhibition
Halls

World Trade
Centre

S'pore
Maritime
Showcase

Road N

West Wharf

Road Q

East Wharf

East Lagoon

Keppel Channel

Regional Ferry

Singapore
Cruise Centre

Tg.
Rimau

P. RENGGIS

**Underwater
World**

Fort
Siloso

Mt. Siloso

Nature Walk
Dragon Trail

Ruined City &
Lost Civilization

Shangri-La's
Rasa Sentosa
Resort

Siloso Beach

Mt. Imbiah

Asian
Village

Cable
Car Station

Merlion
Tower

NTUC Sentosa Beach
Resort

Butterfly Park &
World Insectarium

Pioneers of S'pore
Surrender Chambers

Wonder Golf

Campsite

**Food Village
Central Lagoon**

Playground

Pasar Malam

Canoe Centre

Beaufort
Resort

Brani Terminal
Building

Brani Terminal Avenue

Brani Terminal Avenue

P. BRANI

CAUSEWAY
BRIDGE

Maritime
Museum

Youth
Hostel

SENTOSA

Serapong
Golf
Course

Mt. Serapong

Serapong
Golf Course

Lake

**BURAN
DARAT**

Serapong Golf
Course

Telok

Keppel Channel

Selat Sengkir

Sentosa
Golf Club

Tanjong Golf Course

Tanjong
Beach

Durian

SENTOSA

❶ Fountain Gardens ❻ Pasar Malam
❷ Musical Fountain ❼ Fantasy Island
❸ VolcanoLand ❽ Roller Skating
❹ Orchid Gardens ❾ Plant Nursery
❺ Rasa Sentosa ❿ Art Centre

54

50

46

Welcome to

Singapore is hot! Not just because it is nearly on the equator, but because of all that's happening here. This proud nation strides confidently into the 21st century.

Above: Singapore's National Day Parade, a source of great national pride, takes place each August on the Padang (Malay for plain or field) near City Hall, Parliament House, the Supreme Court and other important civic buildings.
Right: Looking north west across the city, the land in the right foreground is reclaimed from the sea, like much of Singapore's easterly fringes. The tall buildings form the financial district of Shenton Way and Robinson Road, while the East Coast Parkway snakes across the landscape.

f OR A COUNTRY that gained full independence as recently as 1965, Singapore has come a long way. Legend has it that the island once known as Temasek was settled back in the mists of time by Sri Tri Buana, who established Singapura—Lion City— after he sighted a leonine beast in the area. His descendants ruled for five generations until the last ruler, Parameswara, was forced to flee when the Javanese attacked. The first documentary evidence for Singapore dates from the thirteenth century, when it was a flourishing centre for trade. A slow decline followed, with jungle reclaiming the island. By the nineteenth century, seafarers who roamed the region had created a few settlements on the island, and some enterprising Chinese migrants established plantations of gambier and pepper. But the arrival of one man would change everything.

the New Asia!

t o COUNTER THE DUTCH TRADING monopolies in the East, Sir Thomas Stamford Raffles signed an agreement with the Sultan of Johor, allowing the British to establish a trading post on Singapore. Thus began Singapore's modern era. Within three years of Raffles' landing in 1819, the population numbered more than 10,000, of which 60 per cent were Malays. By 1860, at the first census, the population exceeded 80,000 and was mostly Chinese. Other migrants seeking success included Tamils, Ceylonese, Bengalis, Gujuratis, Punjabis, Javanese, Bugis, Balinese and Sumatrans, as well as Europeans. The foundations were laid for Singapore's remarkable growth.

Above: Many tall buildings in Singapore are Housing & Development Board (HDB) apartment blocks, home to 85 per cent of the population.
Left: Part of an ever-expanding network of expressways.
Facing page: Although no longer a regular means of transport, a trishaw ride is still popular with tourists.

$\mathcal{A}$FTER RAFFLES, Singapore prospered for many years under the British. In 1929, however, tin and rubber prices collapsed and thousands lost their jobs in the Great Depression. Although considered impregnable by the Allies during the Second World War, Singapore was quickly overrun by the Japanese in 1942. After peace in 1945, Singaporeans began planning for independence. Under a new constitution David Marshall was elected first chief minister in 1955, and he lobbied Britain unsuccessfully for full independence. Meanwhile a young Straits-born Cambridge graduate led a group of lawyers, teachers and journalists in forming a left-wing political party whose rallying cry was *"Merdeka!"* (freedom). In the 1959 elections, Lee Kuan Yew and his People's Action Party swept to power. After failing in an attempt to become a Malaysian state in 1963, Singapore became fully independent in 1965. Lee became the first prime minister, and stayed in that position for 31 years, stepping aside in 1990 into the specially created position of senior minister to allow a younger generation to take the political reins. His vision, intellect and integrity have earned him a place in history.

Far left: National Day parade taking place in the deepening twilight.

Above left: The Mass Rapid Transit (MRT) system serves most HDB estates and New Towns. It is soon to be augmented by a Light Rapid Transit (LRT) system.

Left: Singapore Art Museum is housed in a beautifully restored school building, the former St Joseph's Institution, which was the first Catholic school in Singapore.

Below: Most of the world's major players in banking and finance maintain a significant presence in Singapore and it is likely that their offices will be found here in the downtown financial district, overlooking the waterfront.

From top: Elgin Bridge and the Singapore River; Cruise Centre and one of the cable car towers, with a cable car heading for Sentosa Island; cruising on the river is popular now that the waterway has been largely turned over to leisure usage.

POST-COLONIAL SINGAPORE is an astonishing success story. The People's Action Party, in power to this day, began alleviating poverty early. Infrastructure has always been a high priority. Low-cost, high-rise housing replaced over-crowded downtown areas, and most Singaporeans now own their homes. The container port is one of the world's busiest and most efficient. The Mass Rapid Transit system is the envy of other nations. Business travellers consistently rate Changi Airport the best in the world. Manufacturing industries fuelled much of the annual growth of eight per cent or so over many years, aided by the famous Chinese work ethic. Tourism, too, has been encouraged and is a thriving industry.

Right: Siloso Beach on Sentosa Island, Singapore's very own holiday isle.

Below: The soaring downtown skyscrapers overlook the river's restored shophouses and godowns, many of which have been transformed into popular eating and drinking spots, where colleagues mingle socially after a typically long day's work.

a dynamic
melting pot
of cultures

Since the Sixties, Singapore has been a peaceful, multicultural society composed of Chinese, Malays, Indians, Eurasians and others.

WHO ARE THE SINGAPOREANS? Early in the nineteenth century, Malays formed the majority of Singapore's population. Now the balance has shifted and Singapore is the only country where Overseas Chinese are in a majority. They form 77 per cent of the population, followed by Malays (14 per cent) and Indians (7 per cent), with Eurasians, Westerners and others making up the balance. You can hear people speaking Hokkien, Mandarin, Cantonese, Teochew, Malay (still the official national tongue and the language of the national anthem), Tamil, Hindi, Portuguese and English…not to mention Singlish, the local dialect, which blends Chinese and Malay words with English. Such diversity makes for a fascinating mixture of cultures.

Clockwise from right: Young people view participation in the National Day parade as good citizenship; every section of society is represented, including the police; you must look your best on the most important day of the year; there is pomp, but it is also a time of great happiness.

Clockwise from left: Near Serangoon Road, Chinese chess players battle it out on a five-foot way, as sidewalks are still occasionally known in Singapore; the ambition of these Muslim boys will be to earn the right to wear the white headwear as adults that indicates they are *Haji*, men who have undertaken the all-important pilgrimage to Mecca; trend-setting clearly began at an early age for this young Chinese boy; these Peranakan women are wearing traditional *sarung kebaya* (Malay for sarong and blouse). Peranakan is a term for persons of mixed Malay and Chinese descent.

Above: St Andrew's Cathedral, which faces Raffles City shopping centre, has been the home of Anglicanism in Singapore since construction was completed in 1861.

Centre left: During the Thaipusam festival, Hindus whose prayers have been answered throughout the year, give thanks by living cleanly and piercing their cheeks and other parts of the body with iron needles. They make a pilgrimage to the temple, while carrying *kavadis*, heavy structures whose weight is transferred to the carrier by steel skewers which pierce the penitent's flesh.

Centre right: This 15-metre-high golden statue of the Buddha is in the Temple of 1,000 Lights, in Little India.

Right: Sultan Mosque on North Bridge Road is a focal point for Muslims, who are virtually all Malay in Singapore. There has been a mosque on the site since 1824, and the present one dates from 1928.

P EOPLE, WHO CAME TO SETTLE in Singapore from many lands, often brought their religious beliefs and philosophies with them. More than half the people are Buddhist, Taoist or Confucianist. About 15 per cent profess the Islamic faith, and a similar percentage are Christians. Three or four per cent are Hindus. Of course, some Singaporeans do not follow any religion and, if asked, describe themselves as free-thinkers. In a tiny nation (a little over 600 square kilometres) with such a mixture of beliefs, keeping the peace has not always been easy, and parliament has passed laws to ensure religious and cultural harmony. Observing weddings, funerals and other ceremonies is one way to gain an insight into other people's belief systems, and Singaporeans of varying beliefs happily attend each other's rites of passage and special feast days.

a land of many beliefs

Buddhists, Christians, Muslims, Hindus and others have learned to live side by side, tolerant of each other's very different religious beliefs.

Above: Many Chinese people believe that lighting huge joss sticks, burning paper money, placing roadside food offerings and holding noisy opera performances during the Festival of Hungry Ghosts appeases the souls of the dead, said to roam the streets in the seventh month of the lunar calendar.
Right: The Hindu goddess Siva dancing on the back of Nadi, the bull. This manifestation of Siva is known as Nadaraja.

singapore's rich colonial heritage

Singapore has preserved many important colonial buildings.

T HE COLONIAL HISTORY of Singapore began in 1819 when Raffles landed. Many early buildings were designed by Irish architect George Coleman, who consulted with Raffles on the Town Plan of 1822–23. Several of his buildings remain, including the charming Armenian Church. The other great architect of the colonial period was the Englishman Alfred John Bidwell, whose work included the original main wing of the Raffles Hotel, Goodwood Hotel, Stamford House, Singapore Cricket Club

Left: The man whose name is everywhere you turn, Sir Thomas Stamford Raffles.
Below: Raffles Hotel was restored—some say rebuilt—as recently as the Eighties at a cost of US$200 million.
Right: Near Raffles is Chijmes, an acronym for Convent of the Holy Infant Jesus, recently developed as an upmarket retail and leisure complex.

and Victoria Theatre. Between them, these two men created the finest colonial architecture in the region. The Padang is the centre for several fine buildings, including the Cricket Club, Supreme Court, City Hall, old Parliament House and Victoria Theatre. Many historic buildings have been lost, however, in the race for economic prosperity since independence. Whole neighbourhoods were destroyed, although critics should not forget that much of the housing torn down was cramped and insanitary. Conservation efforts began in 1970 with the passing of the Preservation of Monuments Act, followed in 1973 by the Urban Redevelopment Act. While Bugis Street (which was moved 300 metres!) and Little India have been criticised, preservation work at Boat Quay, the former St Joseph's Institution (now Singapore Art Museum), Empress Place and elsewhere has been highly praised.

Clockwise from left: The old, represented by the MPH book store on Stamford Road, and the new are often in stark contrast in Singapore; a handful of important colonial buildings survives around the city-centre field known as the Padang; these sculptures outside the National Museum always attract comment; a fountain in the grounds of Raffles Hotel; Victoria Theatre; the doorman at Raffles is one of the most photographed people in Singapore.

exploring
the singapore
river

Singapore River has witnessed many important events in the country's history.

dECAYING HUMAN SKULLS, apparently left by roving Malay pirates, littered the banks of the Singapore River when Raffles and company stepped ashore on January 29, 1819. Later the river saw wave after wave of immigrant labour arrive from China and elsewhere. For many years the river was also the main avenue of transportation to the city for goods brought into the harbour. Merchants became wealthy and built combined business premises and homes, called shophouses, on its banks. Gradually the river

went into commercial decline as the deepwater port was developed, leaving the river to small craft such as *twakow*, in use until 1983. Now, over 160 years after Raffles left Singapore (he died of a brain tumour three years later in London, at the age of 44), the river has been transformed by restoration and change of use and the shophouses have been converted to bars, restaurants and shops. Boat Quay was the first area to undergo major renovation, and Clarke Quay was also a great success. For visitors and locals alike, the river is now the hub of a vibrant social scene. On Singapore's balmy tropical evenings nothing is more pleasant than wining and dining with friends beside the river.

Preceding spread: Efforts have been made to preserve some interesting colonial buildings alongside the river.
Top and above: Clarke Quay and Boat Quay are popular dining and entertainment spots, especially at night.
Right: Renovated shophouses.
Facing page: Hey look! We've found yet another statue of Raffles.

the bustling
central business district

Singapore is a major regional financial hub, with most of the activity centring around Raffles Place and Shenton Way.

bUSINESS MAKES SINGAPORE TICK and much of it is done by multinational companies, which have been made very welcome here. Most are American, but others come from Japan, Australia, Great Britain, Germany, France and many other countries. Overseas companies have a number of key foreign workers, who are welcomed for their skills. As well, many Singaporean families employ foreign maids,

since both parents work, and building-site workers from overseas are contracted to maintain the continuing construction boom. Approximately half a million foreign workers can be added to the Singaporean population of 3.5 million, another marker of this tiny country's prosperity. At first the government put the emphasis on manufacturing, and now the electronics sector is critically important

Above: Suntec City is rapidly developing as a business and retail district in its own right.

Facing page: Banking, trading, wheeling and dealing—if it's financial, you will find it all happening in the ultra-modern buildings around Raffles Place.

Clockwise from top: Hurrying to work is the same the world over; Singaporeans have been quick to adopt the use of handphones; these sales promotion girls are a colourful contrast to the corporate blue and white shirts; when the work is done, there is always somewhere pleasant to go and eat with friends; many Singaporeans own stocks and shares and are keen to keep an eye on how their investments are performing.
Facing page: Even in the heart of the business district, the volume of traffic is never too great, thanks to stringent controls on the number of vehicles on the road; Far East Square is one of the more recent of many developments in Chinatown.

to the economic health of the nation. Companies making items such as computer chips and disk drives employ thousands of skilled and semi-skilled workers. Singaporeans today tend to be well educated, with many gaining degrees overseas and returning home to good jobs. Banking, finance and other service industries such as advertising have become important sectors as well. The statistics are impressive. Singapore has a per capita annual income in excess of US$23,000—one of the world's highest. It has no foreign debt—indeed it has reserves of about S$124 billion. There is generally full employment. Most working citizens must contribute, along with their employer, towards their own retirement fund, called the Central Provident Fund. The CPF is also used to make mortgage payments, pay for hospitalisation and cover certain other important expenses.

orchard road

the shoppers' paradise

A country lane with nutmeg and pepper orchards became Asia's most famous shopping boulevard.

Clockwise from above: The menswear department of a Japanese department store; Orchard Road/Scotts Road junction; across Orchard is Paterson Road; a local architect designed Ngee Ann City shopping centre in the form of an ocean liner.

Clockwise from right:
Computer terminals in these kiosks on the street will help you find information on everything from hotels to theatre shows; Japanese tourists enjoy a stroll along Scotts Road; sidewalk coffeeshops have become very popular in recent years; just a couple of hundred metres from the bustle of Orchard Road are these beautifully restored houses on peaceful Emerald Hill.

ODAY, EVERYONE ASSOCIATES Orchard Road with shops, but within living memory it was little more than a quiet country lane, complete with tigers. Big changes began in 1958 when Tang Choon Keng moved his C.K. Tang store from River Valley Road. Now, just as in New York's Fifth Avenue and London's Bond Street, you can see the world's top brand names, in exotically-named shopping centres like Lucky Plaza, Wisma Atria, The Heeren and Plaza Singapura. Undoubtedly, Orchard Road is Asia's top address for shopping and people-watching.

Left: The major shopping centres in Singapore compete hard with each other to draw the crowds, and Centrepoint has been consistently successful at this.

Below: Goodwood Park Hotel, which began life in 1900 as the Teutonia Club for Germans in Singapore, is decorated imaginatively for the Christmas season.

the charms of
chinatown

Chinatown was established by early immigrants who came ashore from cramped junks after the hard journey from China.

Facing page: Restored shophouses in Chinatown.
This page from top: A pomelo fruit seller; a performer makes up for her role in a Chinese opera; some local streets have been made pedestrian precincts.

tODAY, THE EARLY CHINESE immigrants would recognise almost nothing of the Chinatown they founded last century. Stepping ashore after sailing in junks from China, they settled in the couple of square kilometres just south of the river. They worked as indentured labourers in harbourside warehouses or on rubber plantations until they had paid off the cost of their passage. Some then became hawkers, tailors or jewellery-makers, industries that still survive in Chinatown. At Thian Hock Keng temple, the Temple of Heavenly Happiness, the Hokkien immigrants gave thanks for a safe journey. The present temple was built on the site of the original one in 1840—and is itself being extensively renovated. That's the

story of Chinatown, where entire streets are being restored or rebuilt. Miraculously the area still has an atmosphere worth savouring, and enough historical buildings remain to make it fascinating. Unless a sign says Fixed Price, you can bargain on the price of goods for sale in the crowded, noisy streets; you can see fortune tellers, medicine men, calligraphers and temple mediums; and you can peek into a Chinese medicine hall or a shop selling paper money for burning during prayers. A keen sense of smell will detect the curious aromas which drift along the sidewalk. In the midst of all this Chinese culture, as if to flout the spirit of Raffles, who in his City Plan divided the city's quarters along racial lines, are mosques and Hindu temples, including the Sri Mariamman temple on South Bridge Road where a fire-walking ceremony called Thimithi takes place each year.

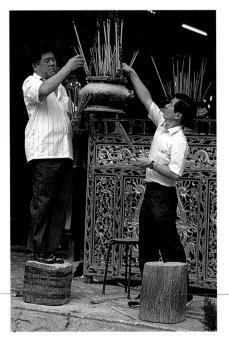

Facing page from top:
Chinatown is busier than ever during the Chinese New Year festival; dried goods on sale include snakes and fish; praying at a Chinese temple; the temple on Telok Ayer Road.
Clockwise from right: Ann Siang Hill; somewhere to hang the laundry; a calligrapher at work; Chinese barbecued pork is a special treat.

Indian immigrant workers, brought in by the British, settled this area in the early nineteenth century.

little india

From top: An Indian fortune-teller awaits customers; Indian women in saris; a South Indian-style wedding takes place in Sri Veerama Kaliamman temple on Serangoon Road—onlookers are often welcomed in to witness ceremonies like this.
Facing page: Sri Sreenivasa Hindu temple on Serangoon Road is dedicated to the god Vishnu.

Serangoon road is the madly pulsing artery running through the heart of Little India. Indian workers first settled the area after the British brought them here to construct famous landmarks like St Andrew's Cathedral, City Hall and The Istana (now the president's official residence). Indians grazed cattle here, too, for the feed was good. Street names evoke history: Buffalo and Kerbau (Malay for buffalo), Hindoo, Veerasamy, Klang (its variant, kling, is a derogatory term for South Indians), together with names of colonists such as the butcher Desker, and heroes of the

empire such as Clive, Campbell and Kitchener, who all played major roles in India rather than Singapore. A walk through Little India today can be an assault on the senses—all of them at once! The area is generally crowded, especially on Sundays when the foreign construction workers have their only day off. Here they gather in huge numbers, and you may have to jostle for space on the sidewalk. There is much to see that is colourful, from sari-clad or Punjabi-suited women to the ornate Hindu temples. The aromas on every corner are those of India—spices, fruits, incense. It's a noisy place, full of unrestrained life. The very best time of year to visit Little India is during Deepavali, the Festival of Lights, when Serangoon Road is awash with colourful lights and happy people.

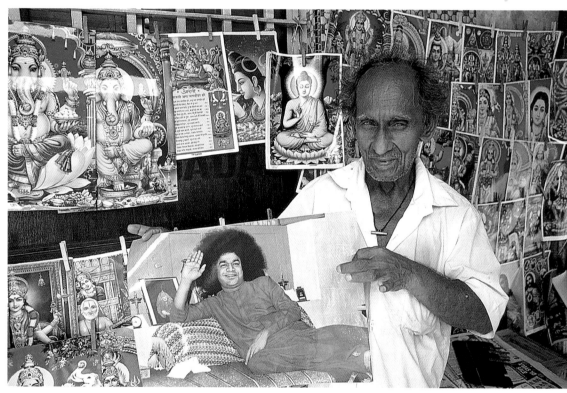

From top: Sri Veerama Kaliamman temple is dedicated to the goddess Kali, the ferocious consort of Siva; a seller of religious art displays a poster of one of Hinduism's great sages, while in the background are posters of Ganesh, the elephant god, and others; a jeweller at work on Serangoon Road.

Far left: The procession for the Thaipusam festival wends its way towards the temple. Left: a woman raises her hands, palms together, in the traditional manner of greeting. Below: A grocery shop in Little India—be sure to step inside, for stores like these exude the most delightful aromas.

Singapore is one of the world's most densely populated countries, averaging about 5,000 residents per square kilometre. The Botanic Gardens, therefore, are even more of a national treasure than in most other cities. Their 50 hectares provide a massive swathe of very welcome green space close to the city centre. The gardens are bounded by Holland Road where it becomes Napier Road, Tyersall Avenue, Tyersall Road, Bukit Timah Road and Cluny Road. The gardens' creation in 1859 was an act of great foresight by colonial figures such as Laurence Niven, the owner of a nearby nutmeg plantation (a few years later disease would end all nutmeg cultivation on Singapore). He supervised the gardens' layout and the clearing of the jungle, where tigers still roamed. One of the interesting characters associated with the Botanic Gardens was their director from 1888 to 1912,

From top: In the Botanic Gardens, as elsewhere in Singapore, somewhere shady and secluded is always at hand; just looking at these water lily ponds is enough to cool you down; a purple water lily in bloom; traditional tai chi exercises; a small reminder of the jungle that once covered Singapore.

botanic gardens

Surprisingly for one of the world's mostly densely populated countries, more than thirty per cent of Singapore is green space.

Sir Henry Ridley, known by some as "Mad Ridley" for his evangelistic promotion of the rubber industry, then in its infancy. He developed a new way to tap latex that didn't kill the tree, and within two decades the Malay Peninsula supplied half the world's latex. Among the gardens' many attractions are orchid pavilions, spice gardens, an eco-lake and occasional concerts. Further from the city centre, there are many more green spaces. Jogging, bird-watching, fishing and cycling are a few of the activities people enjoy at places like Bukit Timah Nature Reserve, MacRitchie Reservoir Park (where there are warning signs about crocodiles), Bishan Park and East Coast Park. At some spots—not especially remote—huge troupes of monkeys can be seen; Upper and Lower Pierce reservoirs are examples. There are also several offshore islands to explore, such as Pulau Ubin. Singapore's claim to be a tropical city of excellence seems especially true after spending time in beautiful areas like these.

From top: An orange orchid in Mandai Orchid Gardens; he's seeking inspiration, perhaps— Singaporeans love orchids and those few home-owners who are fortunate enough to have a garden often grow them; two children pose in the Botanic Gardens.

Clockwise from left: Countless shades of green are enjoyed by visitors, who sensibly use umbrellas to keep the fierce sun at bay; the Orchid Garden within the Botanic Gardens is a year-round attraction; a yellow hibiscus adds a splash of colour to the surrounding greenery.

the singapore & night safari

This zoo, one of the world's finest and newest,
is home to many rare and endangered species,
free to roam in open areas.

SINGAPORE ZOO WAS OPENED as recently as 1973. Now rated among the best in the world, it had its origins in the Sixties when families of British Forces pulled out after independence and left many animals behind. About 40 endangered creatures are among the zoo's 2,000 animals representing some 250 species. Singapore Zoo joins international breeding programmes for rare animals, and one recent surprise was the birth here of a polar bear. The zoo's 100 hectares allow many of the animals to be kept in mini-habitats of open enclosures bounded by rock walls and moats, rather than in barred cages. As well as regular feeding times throughout the day for several groups of animals, attractions such as Children's World, playgrounds and the miniature railway cater especially to the interests of younger people.

Above: Red langur monkeys and other animals and birds can be observed at very close quarters from the zoo's Treetops Trail, a wooden walkway six metres off the ground.
Right: The Komodo dragon is a rare species of monitor lizard found on only a few islands in Indonesia. These carnivores grow up to three and a half metres long, weigh as much as 130kg, and use their poisonous saliva to help overcome large prey such as deer.

Facing page: Many people enjoy interaction with animals, and at the zoo it is possible to ride on an elephant, pose for photographs with an orang utan, meet farmyard animals, and, by booking in advance, take breakfast or afternoon tea with orang utans. Among its many other endangered species, the zoo maintains the world's largest colony of orang utans in captivity as part of its six-island Primate Kingdom attraction.

ZOO

Top: The Night Safari, the first of its kind anywhere, allows visitors to see nocturnal and other animals in action under subdued lighting resembling moonlight. Several types of habitat have been created within the Night Safari's 40 hectares, from African-style savannah to tropical rainforest. It is home to more than 1,200 animals and birds. Listen for the eerie roaring of the big cats. The Night Safari, which is conveniently located next to the zoo, is open from 7.30pm until midnight, and you can even enjoy dinner there before setting out on your safari.

Right: A polar bear, kept suitably cool, is a strange sight in the zoo given Singapore's usual climate of 30 degrees centigrade above rather than 30 degrees below freezing.

Right: A rare Sumatran tiger. Due to hunting and loss of habitat, few survive in the wild.

Facing page: Mandai Orchid Gardens, also near the zoo, is well worth a visit. The business exports millions of orchid sprays worldwide every year.

the mandai orchid gardens

Orchids are a passion in tropical Singapore. The deep-pink and white variety named Vanda Miss Joaquim is the national flower. Orchids have been grown on the Mandai site since 1951, commercially since 1956. The owners of Mandai Orchid Gardens developed the technology that allows these fragile flowers to be exported without damage, and now millions of sprays are sent overseas every year. A morning visit, perhaps before going to the zoo nearby, is best to appreciate the fragrance of these exotic plants. The four-hectare gardens include a landscaped water garden.

the jurong bird

THE JURONG BIRD PARK is extraordinary even by Singaporean standards. It's a 20-hectare home to more than 8,000 birds from 600 species, many of whom fly free in a two-hectare walk-in aviary that features a 30-metre-high man-made waterfall. The various bird shows are enjoyable to watch, but best of all is simply to stroll and keep your eyes open. If you become tired, hop aboard the monorail for a trip through the trees, complete with informative commentary.

From top: Parrots at Jurong Bird Park seem to enjoy mixing with people, and in one of the shows can be seen riding miniature bicycles; the park has a successful breeding colony of flamingoes; birds of prey are put through their paces in these exciting shows, much to the delight of the audience.

This sprawling 20-hectare park, served by a monorail, has more than 600 species of birds from all over the world.

park

Right: Several species of crane live in the park, including this crowned crane. It is a delight to watch their graceful courtship ritual, which has been compared to ballet.
Below: White pelicans, one of a handful of pelican species that reside in the park, like to live in large groups and they fish cooperatively.

the chinese & japanese gardens

LINKED BY THE Bridge of Double Beauty, these two gardens are peaceful havens for city-dwelling Singaporeans. The Chinese Garden features several pagodas, including one styled after the Beijing Summer Palace. The Herb Garden and the Garden of Fragrance are delightful. Also called "The Garden of Tranquillity", the Japanese Garden has stone lanterns, trimmed shrubs and a miniature waterfall. Its classical features also include summerhouses and zen rock gardens.

These traditional gardens provide havens of tranquillity on two huge islands in Jurong Lake.

Right: Lanterns in the shape of Merlions are hung in the Chinese Garden during the mid-autumn Lantern Festival. The Merlion is half fish, half lion, and it was created by the tourism authorities in 1964 as a national symbol for Singapore.
Below: The serene and more simply laid out Japanese Garden was inspired by the fine classical Japanese gardens of the 15th–17th centuries.
Facing page from top: These pagodas in the Chinese Garden are in the Sung Dynasty style—the lights in the background are from government apartment blocks; a tea-house in the Chinese Garden provides shady relief from the blazing sun on a hot day; peaceful scenes like this are frequently the chosen setting for a young couple's wedding costume photographs.

Singapore constantly re-invents itself. In the 1980s the cemetery isle of Pulau Belakang Mati was renamed Sentosa and turned into a tourist park.

sentosa
an island resort

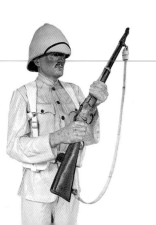

S ENTOSA WAS NOT ALWAYS the carefree resort island it is today. In the 1880s, the British built Fort Siloso on the western tip of the island, known then as Pulau Belakang Mati (poetically, "the island where death lurks behind"). The fort, intended to protect Singapore Harbour, was strategically unimportant until the Second World War, the island's darkest

Top: Sentosa's monorail passes ethnic sculptures as it whisks visitors around the island.
Above: Sentosa offers some fine views of Singapore city.
Facing page: The 11-storey Merlion has an elevator so visitors can take in the views. At night fibre-optic and laser lighting change its colour.

hour. The Japanese attack came not from the sea as expected, but from Malaya. Singapore was taken and the Japanese turned Fort Siloso into a prisoner-of-war camp. The island, appropriately renamed Sentosa ("peace" in Malay), was relaunched in the Eighties as a major tourist drawcard. Fort Siloso is now a museum. Underwater World, Volcano Land, Wonder Golf Park, the Asian Village, Butterfly Park, Fantasy Island water theme park and many other attractions compete for your dollar. Getting around by monorail is a pleasure, although if you are feeling energetic you can always hire a bike. Sentosa is a great place to escape high-stress Singapore.

Left from top: Enjoying a game of volleyball on Sentosa's Siloso Beach, one of three such pleasure beaches on the island; the Musical Fountain at night, with the massive Merlion in the background, is transformed by colour; works of art such as this use fountains and mosaic sculpture to striking effect.
Right: The cablecar from Mount Faber is the most scenic approach to Sentosa.
Below: Underwater World provides a thrilling encounter with sharks, stingrays and scores of other denizens of the deep, which glide overhead.

singapore feasts

SINGAPOREANS, it is said, do not eat to live, they live to eat. That's a good policy in a nation with, arguably, the finest food in the world, and excellent value for money, too. It is still possible to eat well at hawker centres for a few dollars. At the other end of the scale are top restaurants at $100 a head. No single dish defines Singaporean food, since the country's cuisine has been drawn from many lands: China, India, Indonesia, Malaysia, and the best of the West. Famous dishes to try include *nasi lemak* (a staple Malay breakfast), fish-head curry,

Left: Peranakan (or Nonya) food is a spicy cuisine that evolved when Malay and Chinese people began to intermarry in the 1800s.
Below: Cantonese dishes. Chinese cuisine in Singapore consists mainly of Hokkien, Hainanese, Teochew and Cantonese dishes.

Many people—locals and visitors alike—say the food here is the finest in the world. Who's arguing?

Facing page: Frying *dosai*, which are light South Indian pancakes made from a fermented rice and dhal batter.
This page from top: Chilli crabs are a natural favourite for an island nation, and seafood restaurants are popular places to entertain friends and business associates; satay sticks of chicken and other meats are served with a delicious peanut sauce dip; for good, cheap food it is still hard to beat the traditional hawker centres found in every corner of Singapore; outlets of Kopitiam offer hawker food in comfortable, air-conditioned premises.

Hainanese chicken rice, chilli crab, satay, roti prata (Indian bread with curry, a great way to start the day), and Hokkien fried noodles. Of course, you must then sample the great tropical fruits: mango, jackfruit, the spiky durian (if you can stand the smell!), pomelo (like a huge, sweet grapefruit), mangosteen, and so on. Or try a famous local dessert. Many have shaved ice as their base. Ice kacang (ice mountain) includes red beans and sweet syrup among its colourful ingredients. Chendol has red beans, coconut milk and brown sugar. Bubur chacha and bubur hitam both feature sweet potato, yam and coconut milk. Barley-rich chng tng is delicious hot and cold. All this, preferably, in the company of friends, family or colleagues, for eating in Singapore is invariably a social activity.

Facing page: Boat Quay, with its renovated shophouses, is now one of several top nightspots in Singapore.
Clockwise from top: Sugar, in the increasingly happening Mohamad Sultan Road, is one of Singapore's hot new venues in a street lined with boutique pubs and clubs; Alban, lead singer of the group Tania, performs in Anywhere, a club in Tanglin Shopping Centre; Sparks, in Ngee Ann City, is one of the few discotheques in town with staying power.

singapore swings!

The Lion City is not exactly famous for its nightlife, but when the sun goes down Singapore often transforms into Swingapore.

Singapore is becoming funkier by the hour, it seems. This little island nation offers bars and dining by the river as well as big discotheques such as Zouk, Sparks, Top Ten in Orchard Towers, Sugar, and the long-running Fire in Orchard Plaza. Between them, they appeal to all tastes, with customers ranging from young teenagers wearing the latest designer-label clothing to middle-aged men and women. Many of the clubs run special themed parties when people really get into the spirit of things. Besides Orchard Road, there are pubs and clubs in the restored shophouses of Tanjong Pagar, in a relocated and cleaned-up Bugis Street, trendy Holland Village and Mohamad Sultan Road. The zoo, however, offers Singapore's wildest nightspot—the Night Safari.

Contents page (top left) and this page: Telok Ayer Festival Market mural details.
Front endpaper: *Esplanade and Padang*, an oil painting by A.L. Watson of the Padang in the early 1900s.
Back endpaper: *Clarke Quay*, a pen and ink drawing by English artist Peter Goodhall showing the area around 1893.

Front cover, clockwise from top left: Raffles; Traveller's Palm along Boat Quay; Westin Stamford Hotel dwarfs Raffles
Back cover, from top: A Chinese boy; sailing through the dragon in Haw Par Villa theme park; the fountain at Suntec City.
Title page: Girl holding the flag of Singapore.

Published by Periplus Editions (HK) Ltd

Copyright © 2000 Periplus Editions (HK) Ltd.

ISBN 962-593-207-0

Distributors:
Asia Pacific
Berkeley Books Pte Ltd
130 Joo Seng Road, #06-01/03
Singapore 368357
Email: inquiries@periplus.com.sg

North America, Latin America & Europe
Tuttle Publishing
364 Airport Industrial Park
North Clarendon, VT 05759-9436
Tel: (802) 773-8930; Fax: (802) 773-6993
Email: info@tuttlepublishing.com
www.tuttlepublishing.com

Japan
Tuttle Publishing
Yaekari Building, 3rd Floor
5-4-12 Osaki, Shinagawa-ku, Tokyo 141-0032
Tel: (03) 5437-0171; Fax: (03) 5437-0755
Email: tuttle-sales@gol.com

Publisher: Eric M. Oey
Designers: Nicholas Blosch, Jeffrey Ang
Project editor: Michael Stachels
Writer: David Blocksidge
Principal photographer: Ingo Jezierski
Cartography: Violet Wong

Photographic Credits

Antiques of the Orient Endpapers
Wendy Chan Front cover (top left), back cover (middle), title page, 5, 6, 7, 8, 9 (middle and bottom), 10 (middle), 11 (bottom), 14 (top middle, right), 15 (middle, bottom left), 19, 22, 23 (bottom), 24 (middle), 32 (bottom left, right), 33 (top), 34, 36 (top left, bottom left), 40 (bottom), 41 (top right, bottom), 47 (top left), 48 (top), 53 (top right), 54 (main picture), 60
Alain Evrard/Photobank 14 (top left, bottom)
Jill Gocher 9 (top), 21 (middle), 46 (bottom), back cover (bottom)
Roger de la Harpe/Photobank 48 (bottom)
Ingo Jezierski Front cover (top right, bottom), 2, 4, 10 (top, bottom), 11 (top), 12, 13, 15 (top, bottom right), 16, 17, 18, 20, 21 (top left, top right, bottom), 23 (top), 24 (bottom), 25, 26, 27, 28, 29, 30, 31 (top), 32 (top, middle right), 33 (bottom), 35, 36 (top right, bottom right), 37, 38, 39, 40 (top, middle), 41 (top left), 42, 43 (inset), 44, 45, 46 (top), 47 (top right, bottom), 48 (middle), 49, 50 (middle, bottom), 51, 52, 53 (top left, bottom), 54 (top, cut-out), 55, 56, 57 (bottom), 61, 62, 63 (bottom left and right), 64, back cover (top)
Jean Kugler/Photobank 31 (bottom), 50 (top)
Peter Mealin 63 (top)
Luca Invernizzi Tettoni/Photobank Front cover (top right), 24 (top), 43 (main picture), 57 (top), 58, 59

Printed in Singapore